Psychotherapy

Thomas Hodge

2014

Table of Contents

Psychoanalytic Stages

and Defenses

Sigmund Freud radical approach to examining mental health changed the way in which mental suffering was understood. Two of his theory's contributions have served deeply impacted the field of psychology for over one hundred years. By emphasizing the development of an individual through psychosexual stages, psychoanalysis provided insight into the way in which prior events in life impact current thought, behavior, and experience. The psychosexual stages have been challenged over the years, but the basic ideal of abnormalities in development serving to explain abnormalities in current functioning has persevered. Various other theorists have made attempts to modify and change the models and stages, but the premise that conflicts in earlier stages influence adult behavior and thought has maintained as a constant in many later models.

In addition to the contribution of a stage theory, psychoanalysis contributed to the understanding psychological processes by noting the presence of defense mechanisms that are used by the ego for protection. Defense mechanisms serve to play off the normal and abnormal resolution and experiences of various stages of development. Maladaptive strategies of defense mechanisms serve to explain many of the abnormal behaviors that have been observed by psychoanalysts. In understanding developmental stages and defense mechanisms, one can develop a strategy and effective approach in bringing these causes for behavior to the attention of a client for the purpose of adjusting the individual's processes of thought. Upon understanding how conflicts in the stages affect the individual and the defense mechanism use, patterns of thought can be modified to produce improvements in functioning.

Psychosexual Stages of Development

Psychoanalysis laid the groundwork for creating a development theory based on the anatomical area that produces pleasure during certain age ranges in development. As an individual progresses through stages, the focus changes from one area of pleasure gain to another anatomical region. Garcia (1995) explained, "The emphasis is not on the passing of the stages but rather on how much of that which is gained at each stage is brought to the next stage to become a permanent part of the character" (p. 500). The impact of the stage is not based on an individual completion of the stage but on the influence of experience gained during the time in that stage. The psychosexual stages are not simply a checklist of phases that are noted as being accomplished. Psychoanalysis explains the stages as the period of time which influence the characteristics and tendencies of the individual throughout life. The experiences during that stage affect the judgment, biases, and decision-making processes of the individual throughout later periods of life.

Pakes (1975) provided connections between numerous psychopathologies and experiences during differing psychosexual stages as the individual having their desires overindulged or neglected. As defined by psychoanalysis, abnormal behavior can be attributed to dependencies that were created due to the influences that impacted the individual during differing stages. Phillips and Framo (1954) explained that the psychosexual development theory allows an understanding of a normal individual and a pathological individual experiencing the same event but from differing perspectives. A normal individual will experience an event in one manner and describe the experience based on how he perceives the event based on his experiences due to how those experiences have shaped his perspective. An individual suffering from a pathological disorder would experience the same event in the same manner but describe the experience in an abnormal manner due to how he perceives the event based on his perception which has been shaped by the experiences during his stages of development which would be different the individual that is of normal functioning.

The psychosexual stage theory of development does have shortcomings in consideration of women and minorities. The psychosexual stage theory has been criticized for its view of women. This is commonly attributed to the concept of penis envy that women experience during the phallic stage. Friedman (1977) described some of the aspects of psychoanalysis that were upsetting to women as being an emphasis on women having a weaker superego and women as being subordinate to men. In examining psychoanalysis' critique of women, one can note that a social occurrence is being noted in explaining penis envy. The concept of penis envy can be understood to explain the desire of women to avoid the oppression that they have experienced while advancing through the psychosexual stages in a male dominated society. Since the society is oppressive to women, a result occurs in which women experience frustrations during the psychosexual stages. This frustrations result in an abnormal development during the stages. Since the abnormalities and frustrations are common throughout the gender, they can be noted as attributing to the differences between the different sexes. The effect that occurs at the subconscious level is penis envy which can manifest in the conscious as rebellious behavior against society and normality.

Defense Mechanisms

In understanding abnormal behavior, psychoanalysis supplements the explanations provided by the psychosexual stage theory with the concept of defense mechanisms. The defense mechanisms serve to aid the individual in coping with unpleasant experiences. Porcerelli, Thomas, Hibbard, and Cogan (1998) explain that defense mechanisms develop as an individual passes through the stages of development and progress from immature mechanisms to more mature and developed mechanisms with age and time. Dysfunctions can occur if an individual progress through life into more advanced stages of development but does not progress to more mature types of defense mechanisms. Since denial is one of the most primitive forms of defense mechanisms, utilizing denial at later stages of life become problematic resulting difficulties for the individual to effectively cope with different experiences in adult life due to underdeveloped and overused defense mechanism strategies. In this manner, defense mechanism serve to be ineffective in protected the ego from dangers and actually become harmful to the individual.

In addition to defense mechanisms serving to aid in explaining psychopathology, defense mechanisms are aided in explaining how individuals function in a normal manner. In contrast to maladaptive defense strategies, properly adaptive strategies can direct a therapist in understanding healthy ways in which an individual can cope with perceived threats to the ego. Scano (2007) explained that defenses also served as aids in structuring experiences for the individual in addition to resulting in pathology. Structuring experiences of a defense mechanism can clearly be noted in the function of memory repression. Memory repression allows an individual to function in a normal manner without being overwhelmed by memories of past experiences that would inhibit his ability to function successfully as required by current activities. Repression allows for protection of the ego from a flood of emotions and irrelevant memories that would be used by the superego to produce fear and anxiety in the ego.

Applications of Theory

In applying the concepts of the psychosexual stage theory and defense mechanisms, psychological difficulties can be more fully understood to allow for the root cause of suffering to be revealed. In revealing the root cause, this allows for a focus of efforts to treat the cause of problems as opposed to simply treating the symptoms. If the cause is addressed in therapy, the effect of treatment would be more likely to be lasting. Clements, Sabourin, and Spiby (2004) describe the causes of dysphoria and hopelessness in abuse victims as being connected to self-blame among the victims. In examining victims of abuse, one can note that events occurred during psychosexual stages of development that resulted in unresolved conflicts. The particular effects would vary from case to case based on the stage of development in which the abuse occurred, but the effects can be noted by the maladaptive use of defense mechanisms. An abuse victim may present a tendency to use denial as an inappropriate defense mechanism which would result in omitting details of the situation as the individual reflects on the event. As details which would defend against self-blame are denied, the ego is unable to use more mature defense mechanisms, such as rationalization, to defend the individual's actions against the accusations and worries of the superego. This pattern leads to low self-esteem and hopelessness.

In therapeutic treatment, the therapist can utilize consciousness raising techniques to allow the individual to become aware of their use of primitive defense mechanisms which have a negative impact more mature mechanisms. Once the client is aware of the harmful effects of the primitive defense mechanism, mature mechanism can become more effective in producing an improved quality of life for the client. In doing this, the client has had a realization as to the patterns of thought that they follow. Using this understanding of thought, the client can also apply the lessons learned from their sessions of psychoanalysis to other situations that they experience to prevent similar psychological suffering occurring as the result of similar process caused in different contexts. In this manner, psychoanalysis is more likely to prevent the recurrence of symptoms in clients as opposed to a treatment that would only treat the symptoms as opposed to the root cause.

Summary

In conclusion, the contributions of psychoanalysis serve to allow for an understanding and effective treatment of psychological suffering which is caused by maladaptive strategies during development through the earlier stages of life. In making the connections between maladaptive development and later psychological suffering, psychoanalysis demonstrates an explanation of the causes that lead to the effects of dysfunctional thought processes. The defense mechanisms serve as a connection between early experiences in life and the function or dysfunction experienced in later life. In using defense mechanism strategies, psychoanalysis not only describes a correlation between early experience in development but also a cause and effect relationship.

In understanding the causes of normal and abnormal strategies, the therapist is able to utilize consciousness raising strategies to correct symptoms of psychological dysfunction. The applications of this approach to psychological processes extend to a wide variety of scenarios and allow for the correct various types of suffering in clients. As the client becomes aware of their own strategies in coping and defending against undesirable experiences, corrections can be in the patterns of thought of the client to allow for improvement in the mindset of the client which can lead to lower likelihood of symptom recurrence and a lasting improvement in life experiences.

Logotherapy

Logotherapy took a radically different approach at examining personality, psychopathology, and therapeutic treatment of individuals. Prior approaches had focused on the biological forces that drive an individual and attempted to explain human behavior, thought, and emotions as being universal in a sense that a stimulus would elicit a specific response. Logotherapy broke away from that line of thinking in that it challenges the concept that human thought, emotion, and behavior must follow a particular reaction to a stimulus. In providing this concept, logotherapy provides a much greater opportunity for improvement in individuals by providing a solution for how one can overcome the circumstances of their life. Logotherapy's greatest strength has often been debated as its greatest weakness which is that each person is unique. As strength, this is used to tailor treatment of each individual to the unique situation of each person. As a weakness, it serves as an opportunity for the approach to be challenged as it can be debated that an approach should fully explain the response of individuals to their environment more precisely as opposed to challenging the notion. In addition, logotherapy is often coupled with a secondary therapeutic approach in treating individuals. As logotherapy is often a supplemental approach, one could perceive its need to be coupled with another approach as a weakness that could de-legitimize logotherapy as a stand-alone therapeutic approach.

In addition to being simply unique, logotherapy provided a perspective that allowed for psychotherapists to consider the purpose or direction of a person's life in therapy as opposed to simply considering biological drives and mechanisms that drove a person. Logotherapy contributed a deep understanding of humans as being more than simply a combination of primal urges and societal clashes. In examining the meaning each individual and humanity as a whole searches, logotherapy serves as a useful technique in treating a wide variety of psychological conditions and also serves to amplify other treatments when used in conjunction with other psychotherapeutic approaches.

Strengths and Weaknesses
of Logotherapy

Das (1998) explained that a loss or dysfunction view of meaning appeared as a common thread across several psychological disorders including depression, anxiety, eating disorders, and obsessive compulsive disorders. One can clearly note that logotherapy's emphasis on meaning serves as an explanation of how that numerous individuals fall into a state of psychological crisis. If one has lost meaning, the loss can create a state of depression for the individual as noted by studies of Koren and Lowenstein (2008) when they examined elderly widows that had lost meaning in life as a result of their loss of a spouse later in life. The individuals had connected their spouses to their meaning for life. Upon the loss, the individuals had developed a feeling that they no longer had a meaning or purpose which led to a depressive state. In the case of anxiety, meaning has a connection to the psychological state of the individuals as it can be noted that the individual feels frustration and confusion at the possibility that they had invested a great deal of time into pursuing a meaning or purpose that was not successful or correct for them to pursue. Das (1998) referred to this type of anxiety being created as one experiences a state of transitoriness in which the individual becomes aware of the brevity of time that they have to discover a meaning or purpose.

In considering the weaknesses of logotherapy, the couple of logotherapy with other approaches could be considered a weakness of the approach. Shrum (2004) demonstrated that logotherapy had an effect on the rehabilitation of inmates, but it was coupled with intensive journaling and other cognitive-based programs. Southwick, Gilmartin, Mcdonough, and Morrissey (2006) described the effects of logotherapy in treating individuals suffering from post-traumatic stress disorder, but they also coupled it with psycho-pharmacological treatment, gestaltist group therapy, and short-term psychotherapy. The manner in which this presents a weakness is that logotherapy couples with other therapies to be effective, but it is not designed to stand on its own as a treatment requiring another therapeutic approach.

In addition to its inability to stand alone as a treatment, one can also attest the same shortfall to logotherapy as psychotherapy had. Logotherapy is very flexible. It can shift as needed to fit different individuals. As a therapy is capable of being altered, it is less likely to be able to be proven as effective or ineffective by scientific measurement. This line of argument serves to show that logotherapy waivers in a manner that demonstrates an inconsistency in its methods.

The two major weaknesses of logotherapy can be easily addressed as strengths of the approach at the same moment. The flexibility of logotherapy demonstrates an approach that is able to be adapted to the differences between individuals. If a therapy is rigorous and unwavering in its application, the approach is unable to be adjusted for different people and is less effective. The coupling of logotherapy with other therapies demonstrates a therapeutic emphasis on increasing the effectiveness of sole treatments by themselves. As it is effective in providing improved results with a variety of proven methods, logotherapy serves as an amplifying force that increases the effectiveness of treatments and decreases the probability of relapse after treatment ceases for individuals.

Applications and Contributions

Logotherapy has demonstrated a high degree of usefulness in a variety of applications. Lantz (1998) applied the approach of logotherapy to group therapy. In examining the effect of the approach on the group, Lantz (1998) found that therapy groups developed a greater degree of cohesiveness and had groups stay together for as long as fifteen years. The impact of logotherapy on a group setting of therapy is that deeper connections are made between group members that seem to be longer lasting. The individuals in a logotherapy group setting utilize several techniques that are very similar to Gestaltist techniques but focus on a deeper meaning for life and the purpose in life of the individuals. The connections that are made between the group members are highly supportive and understanding in these types of group settings due the universality of individuals' desiring a meaning in life and daily activities. Das (1998) addressed the concept of apathy that prevailed throughout society as being something that affected a societal group in having a meaning. The use of logotherapy in group setting demonstrates how the group can combat the pressure of societal apathy upon the individual by providing a supportive network and structure for the individuals of the group.

Logotherapy addresses individual suffering and provides a meaning for the suffering that one experiences. By addressing suffering, logotherapy provides an option for addressing depression. Blair (2004) utilized logotherapy for the treatment of adolescents with depression. In treating the adolescents, he found that the treatment was useful when dealing with individuals that were able to introspectively examine how they felt about their depression and the effects it had upon them. The approach gave the adolescents power to make decisions for themselves by providing them with an opening to insert whatever answer they felt would be correct in understanding their depression instead of needing to choose from the options that were provided to them by external sources that would often conflict each other. As the individuals began to shift focus from suffering without meaning to the meaning in their suffering, their depressive symptoms would alleviate by the fact that the depressive symptoms were not the topic of focus, but the meaning had become the topic of focus for the adolescents.

Summary

In conclusion, logotherapy has contributed to improve the effectiveness of several other therapeutic approaches. In advancing other approaches, logotherapy has shown that a single treatment that does not provide a purpose for an individual to improve or persevere through suffering is not as effective over time as one that also addresses why the individual had suffered through the difficult episodes. To provide a point to the suffering and turmoil allows the individual to more fully understand and respect the situation in which they experience life. To suffering meaninglessly is much worse that to suffer with a purpose. Occasionally, a purpose will pull the individual through the suffering to a better state of mind and condition. Logotherapy aids the individual to understand a reason for their difficulties for the purpose of making sense of life. When everything makes sense and the person understands life a little better, psychological difficulties become a little easier to survive.

Rational Emotive Behavioral Therapy

Rational emotive behavioral therapy (REBT) provides a formative approach to therapy that examines personality, psychopathology, and treatment from a perspective that gives respect to the beliefs of the individuals that create irrational thinking. The attention that REBT gives to the underlying beliefs that create anxiety, depression, and other forms of maladaptive philosophies and beliefs serves as a strength of the approach. The approach serves to be highly adaptive in addressing the uniqueness among human beings by attempting to explain how oppressive views of society can detract from the well being of an individual. In addition to this strength, REBT serves as an approach that is authentic with clients and assists clients in gaining a realistic and rational view of themselves and their environment. Often, others have challenged the hedonistic views of REBT as being neglecting of the cultural expectations and denying of the impacts of environmental pressures. These challenges can be easily refuted though when considering the approach as addressing the well-being of the individual and the approach being looked at as a method of improving the quality of life of individuals. REBT can be seen as useful when working with clients that hold maladaptive expectations of the world and experience difficulties as a result of such expectations and beliefs. In doing so, REBT serves to tie drives that are present in many other approaches such as individual being driven by prior experiences and others being pulled in a direction by goals.

Addressing Beliefs

The focus of REBT is to change the way in which people think about things. This approach addresses the fixations they have about how critical accomplishing certain tasks are to maintaining their psychological well-being. In addressing the rationality of one's beliefs about the things that are important and the degree of importance these beliefs hold on the person, REBT relieves the stress that an individual imposes on himself or herself (Ellis, Shaughnessy, and Mahan, 2002). This can be seen as being tied to the idea of allowing the individual the chance to restructure their meaning in life and importance that they give to their beliefs. As one confronts the connections that have made between their actions and consequences, the burden of expectations and the connection of meaning can be broken by considering things logically.

REBT serves to disrupt the irrational beliefs of an individual by getting the client to inspect the logic of their process. As this process proceeds, the client will confront their process, and the irrational connections that the client has made will be drawn to his attention. A significant impact that this process contains is that it aids the client in understanding how logical thought patterns can exist. As the client sees the difference between logical and illogical patterns of thought, the client can use the same process in developing similar logical patterns in other venues of life (Still, 2006). The change that is produced by REBT is not a change that modifies a single symptom in the person's life and behavior. The change is a systemic change in the person's process of understanding and beliefs. The addressing of the irrational beliefs at the root of the person's suffering in one area of life will ideally free the person from the suffering that is caused by other irrational beliefs that are affecting them in other areas of life.

Authentic and Hedonistic

If a therapist is working with a client and the client feels that therapist is not portraying the therapist's genuine opinion, the client will perceive the therapist as someone who is only attempting to manipulate the client to do his will. REBT therapists present a truly genuine and authentic image to the client. The therapist still provides the client with acceptance but does so in an authentic manner by pointing out to the client when they are being irrational in their beliefs. (Dryden and David, 2008). REBT therapists often use several techniques when providing the client with authentic criticism. The therapist often uses humor and pragmatic arguments in changing the beliefs of the clients from irrational to rational patterns. While confronting the irrationalities of the clients' beliefs, the therapist approaches the issue in a non-judgmental manner that ensures the client is aware of the irrationalities while realizing that the therapist is not judging them (Weinrach et al., 2001).

In addition to being authentic with the client, REBT encourages the client to live a hedonistic lifestyle. The lifestyle is hedonistic in a long-term sense as opposed to a short-term sense. REBT encourages high frustration tolerance and the acceptance of what happens in one's life unconditionally. The view of unconditional acceptance of one's life and self reduces frustrations. With less frustrations, the quality of life increases for the client, and the long-term pleasure is achieved for the individual (Ellis, 2005).

Others have criticized REBT's emphasis on increasing pleasure and decreasing suffering as being an unrealistic approach and grounding for therapy. In confrontation such criticisms, one must consider what the goal of therapy is. Some therapies have focused mainly on treating symptoms and reducing problematic symptoms. Such treatments resolve the specific symptoms by manipulating the individual into presenting contradictory behaviors to the symptoms or delaying the presentation of symptoms. Reducing the presentation of symptoms may appear impressive to others, as the symptoms are what they are looking for and measuring. For the individual that suffers, the problem still exists but often manifests in a different manner. The patient may not think about killing himself due to a recently dissolved relationship, but he may still enter into his next relationship holding the same underlying beliefs that led to his suicidal ideations that were recently resolved by another therapy. REBT confronts the beliefs that reduce the ability of the individual to experience pleasure and increase the likelihood of experiencing the inverse of pleasure. To restructure those beliefs creates more long-term pleasure for the individual and a more long-term solution to the problems that the individual experiences (Ellis, Shaughnessy, and Mahan, 2002).

Individuals that criticize REBT often focus on the hedonistic focus as being negative. The focus has been seen by some as detracting from the need to have the client cooperate with society and the environment. Critics will often consider that if one focus on self-pleasure that they will deny the impacts upon the other members of society. Interestingly, REBT addresses this criticism by the use of logic. If an individual goes against societal norms and expectations to a degree that the society would be so negatively effected, the individual would experience a loss of certain potential pleasure. This turns the reasoning of the critic's argument against itself due to the failure of the argument to consider the issue of long-term hedonism in a rational and contextual manner.

Connections to Other Approaches

REBT can clearly be seen as be similar to several other approaches. The approach seems to be very well integrated with Existential therapy, Humanistic therapy, and Behavioral therapy. The behavioristic therapist would have an easier time accepting REBT than many other therapeutic approaches due to the large base of empirical and scientific support of REBT over the years. The existentialist and humanistic therapists can approach REBT as a more firm approach that can compliment their own approach. REBT provides a therapist with the opportunity to be genuine in a highly constructive manner. This genuineness of the approach and logic allows an opportunity for the therapist to persuade and reason with the client while still being mindful of the client in a respectful manner. This firmness is often needed in some of the humanistic approaches but not fully addressed aside from providing the client with a model by which they can replicate the behavior and mannerisms. The reasoning of REBT provides the therapist a platform by which they can convey the reasoning to the client in a more direct manner than simply hoping that the client will accept the model provided and assume such a model (Weinrach, 1995).

Conclusion

In conclusion, REBT serves as an approach that efficiently addresses not only a single problem for the individual but changes the dysfunctional belief system of the individual into a functional system that improves the quality of life for the person. The confrontation of the illogical patterns of thought disrupts beliefs that lead to suffering and frustration for the person. The approach serves to be authentic in a manner that avoids offending the client and pushing them away from change while still being firm and not enforcing the maladaptive thoughts. Through the advancement logical reasoning, REBT attempts to improve the individual's quality of life in a more long-term fashion as opposed to only being a short-term solution. In focusing on long-term solutions, REBT provides a viable solution that is more positive for all involved parties with therapy and also provides a better outcome for the individuals that are indirectly impacted by the changes in the individual's system of belief. By being so flexible, REBT serves as an approach that can profoundly integrated with various other therapeutic systems to advance the outcome of treatment for the patient consistently.

Various Therapies in Nutshell

Adlerian Therapy

With consideration of Adlerian therapy, one of the most prolific contributions would be Adler's shift from a focus on prior events determining the individual's psychological state to focus on the drive of the individual toward a goal. Freud focused on the past affecting the present while Adler looked at the direction in which an individual is heading. As one comes to realize fictional finalism, the client can then begin to cope with whether that finalism is rational or irrational. The connection between goals and psychological states seems to be much closer of a connection than prior experience and the psychological state of an individual. People act based on purpose, direction, and motivation. Fictional finalisms directly impact all three of these components. Meanwhile, Freud's focus on prior experiences addresses mainly the elements that had an impact on an individual's drive and reasoning behind reaching a certain goal. It could be possible that an individual would still maintain the same fictional finalism even after coming to terms with the prior experiences that led the individual to desire such a fictional finalism.

An extreme example of a finalism effecting

behavior would be an individual abusing pain pills in order to achieve a high. The individual's behavior is more influenced by the desire of achieving the end goal of "getting high" as opposed to past experiences with medications. The attention that Adler gave to a goal-driven perspective allows for easier connection to be made between the actions individuals do and the forces that drive those behaviors or thoughts.

In Adler's approach, he does not neglect the causes that lead to an individual developing such fictional finalism. There is an assumption that individuals strive for levels of superiority. The avoidance of inferiority is what causes an individual to develop finalism as goals that create behaviors and thought processes. In laying out this model of how prior experiences lead to goals that lead to behavior, Adler provides the therapist with an understanding of the process of reasoning that leads to abnormality and discomfort. In understanding this pathway, a therapist is able to identify which parts of the pathway serve to be problematic for the client. Upon identifying the issue, steps can be taken to modify the connections that the client has made through reasoning and re-education which can lead to a change in the client's style of life or understanding.

Existential Void

The existential void is that which is of greatest concern in the existential approach. I feel that the text does not devote nearly enough time to explaining the concept of the void. Once the void is understood, the rest of the concept will fall into place. The void is simply non-existence. To not exist is very difficult to understand. It can be very upset if one attempts to fully grasp this concept of non-existence. In religious terms, the void can be compared to hell or the Jewish concept of Sheol, which translates to the grave. The concept of sensory deprivation (a state in which all stimuli are removed) can be also used as a good understanding of the existential void. Many times, death is used as a metaphor for understanding the void.

As an example, I will use a dark lake for the void. The void is much like a lake because an individual cannot see what is under the water. Staying above the water in this lake is not an option. One only has the option to go under the dark water and into the unknown mystery that lies underneath the surface. One cannot say that which is in the darkness is neither good nor bad because one does not know what is in the darkness of the deep. One looks out across the lake in the darkness of the deep water and that uncertainty is scary. The unknown is frightening. What is in the unknown could be pleasant or terrible, but simply not knowing makes the unknown extremely terrifying. This fear produces anxiety in some, depressing in some, and various other reactions in others. The void must be crossed. It is unavoidable.

To give meaning to the void is to conquer the void. In logotherapy, this is achieved by assigning some purpose to the trials that one goes through to make it through that void of uncertainty. In ascribing meaning to the trials, the turmoil associated with such trials is reduced. Upon making through the void, one emerges on the other side of the lake. On the other side, the individual is a different person. It is possible that they are better, and it is possible that they are worse than before the void. They are simply different and changed by the experience of surviving the void and coming out on the other side in a state of still existing. Once this is understood, the other concepts of existential therapy will make much more sense.

Interpersonal Therapy

In IPT, the concept of role dispute poses an interesting concept. In examining role disputes, one must consider how these disputes originate, or more appropriately, how the incompatible expectations originate. For example, consider a couple with issues of infidelity. An individual does not enter a relationship with the intention of cheating on his or her partner. The problem that leads to this situation begins when the two first meet. Each individual has a list of what they want or need from a pattern in their mind. This list may be something that he or she is aware of or not. Typically, it is not something that is explicitly created by the person. They will also have a list of what they believe the other person expects from them.

So the two people meet and the relationship begins as relationships typically do. It begins with a few white lies by each person and few things each person does a few things to attempt to compensate for their perceived inferiorities as Adler would say. These white lies may not seem like such a big deal at the time but time has a way of magnifying things to larger sizes. Therefore, no one wants to be caught up in a lie even if it is about their own personality. Other lies are told to the partner and the each individual lies to his or herself also. The relationship is begun on a foundation of lies. Each person is living in a world of lies so that the lists are completely checked off and all needs are satisfied. Unfortunately, the art of keeping up with lies is pretty exhausting. The people eventually get tired and the truth comes out. It is never really addressed, but some of the items on the list get unchecked. This creates deficits for the individuals and also creates a longing for the list items to be satisfied again. Over time, the longing grows stronger. Sometimes, the individuals begin to unintentionally and sometimes intentionally search for those items that they are missing. Other times, the individuals simply become bitter toward one another due to feeling that the other might be to blame for their missing those items off of their list.

An interesting approach that I have seen done before with cases such as these is to have the individuals make out their lists of what is important to them in a partner. Once the lists are made out, each will compare their partner to the list to see which are items are checked off and which are missing. After this is done, each person will go down the list of missing items and ask two simple questions about each missing item. First, they should ask if the lack of that attribute will affect how they function as a couple, and secondly, they will ask if the lack of that attribute affects how they care about each other. I have seen the exercise modified for different types of roles and relationships, but it does serve in raising awareness among individuals about interpersonal issues.

Person-centered Approach

The relationship between the client and therapist in Carl Rogers' person-centered therapy seems like a bit of a balancing act, but the strategy seems to have a clear meaning as to why the approach is useful. Rogers lays out six conditions for the relationship which make sense. Most important among these six points seems to be the themes of genuineness, positive regard, and empathy. Genuineness prevents the client from turning against the therapist. If the client believes the therapist to not be sincere, the client will question the therapist's motives and purpose. Therapy sessions would be either become unproductive or counterproductive if the client does not regard the therapist as being straightforward and genuine. In having unconditional positive regard, the therapist is encouraging the client to realize that they do have worth, and this serves as a device by which the client is freed from their conditions of worth that they perceive they must adhere. Empathy (not sympathy) serves to make a connection between the client and therapist. This connection reinforces the effects of the positive regard of therapist to the client. This understanding allows for the client to see that even with their shortcomings in the open the therapist still maintains positive regard. The effect of this reduces the anxieties that have been caused by incongruences between the current state of the client and the client's perceived goal state that is actually seen as a level of worthiness by the client. Through these strategies, person-centered therapy effectively addresses psychological issues in manner that focuses on achieving a better quality of living for the client.

Common Factors

It seems that the common underlying theme of all the therapeutic theories is to manipulate the understanding and thinking of individuals for the purpose of assisting individuals in functioning from day to day. The debate between different theorists seems to be centered around whether or not a specific approach produces positive results. It can clearly be noted that the connections between the various schools of thought seem to be significant when considering first how the therapist forms a relationship with the patient/client to allow for the individual to open up to the suggested change. This dispute among therapists seems to be one of the contributing factors to the creation of so many different schools of thought on psychotherapy. Since each therapy has individuals both attacking and defending it, young therapists entering the field are more apt to feel that they stand a better chance of creating an approach that is unique in some way but still holds similarities to the schools in which they were trained in originally. As this process has been drug out over the course of one hundred years, the number of therapies has grown in a similar pattern to how the field has grown. As new therapies have emerged from individuals who were trained in older schools of psychotherapy, it is clear that certain factors still are relevant in each of the new therapies. These common threads seem to be the things that all parties agree are fundamentally important in psychotherapy.

Expectations and a therapeutic relationship seem to be the two most prolific threads that go throughout all forms of psychotherapy. Any individual that comes to a therapist has some expectations concerning the outcome of the treatment. If there were no expectation or hope for improvement, there would most likely be no attempt for the therapy to be sought out as a treatment in the first place. In the majority of therapies, it seems that positive expectations would result in an improved chance at success. Secondly, the therapeutic relationship serves to be a necessity in any psychotherapy. Without some type of positive relationship, it seems that the client or patient would be more resistant to treatment, and the therapy would be less effective. Due to this fact, a positive relationship consistently appears across different therapies.

References

Blair, R. G. (2004). Helping Older Adolescents Search for Meaning in Depression. Journal Of Mental Health Counseling, 26(4), 333-347.

Clements, C., Sabourin, C., & Spiby, L. (2004). Dysphoria and Hopelessness Following Battering: The Role of Perceived Control, Coping, and Self-Esteem. *Journal of Family Violence, 19*(1), 25-36.

Das, A. K. (1998). Frankl and the realm of meaning. Journal of Humanistic Education & Development, 36(4), 199.

Dryden, W., & David, D. (2008). Rational Emotive Behavior Therapy: Current Status. *Journal of Cognitive Psychotherapy, 22*(3), 195-209. doi:10.1891/0889-8391.22.3.195

Ellis, A. (2005). Why I (really) became a therapist. *Journal Of Clinical Psychology, 61*(8), 945-948. doi:10.1002/jclp.20166

Ellis, A., Shaughnessy, M. F., & Mahan, V. (2002). An Interview With Albert Ellis about Rational Emotive Behavior Therapy. *North American Journal Of Psychology, 4*(3), 355-366.

Friedman, H. J. (1977). Special Problems of Women in Psychotherapy. *American Journal of Psychotherapy, 31*(3), 405.

Garcia, J. (1995). Freud's Psychosexual Stage Conception: A Developmental Metaphor for Counselors. *Journal of Counseling & Development, 73*(5), 498-502.

Koren, C., & Lowenstein, A. (2008). Late-life Widowhood and Meaning in Life. Ageing International, 32(2), 140-155. doi:10.1007/s12126-008-9008-1

Lantz, J. (1998). Viktor Frankl and Interactional Group Therapy. Journal of Religion & Health, 37(2), 93-104.

Pakes, E. (1975). Dependency and Psychotherapy-Developmental Considerations. *American Journal of Psychotherapy, 29*(1), 128.

Phillips, L., & Framo, J. (1954). Developmental Theory Applied to Normal and Psychopathological Perception. *Journal of Personality, 22*(4), 464. doi:10.1111/1467-6494.ep8930377

Porcerelli, J., Thomas, S., Hibbard, S., & Cogan, R. (1998). Defense Mechanisms Development in Children, Adolescents, and Late Adolescents. *Journal Of Personality Assessment, 71*(3), 411.

Scano, G. (2007). Who defends itself from what? Toward a reformulation of the concept of defense. *International Forum of Psychoanalysis, 16*(3), 140-151. doi:10.1080/08037060701302642

Shrum, H. (2004). No Longer Theory: Correctional Practices That Work. Journal of Correctional Education, 55(3), 225-235.

Southwick, S. M., Gilmartin, R., Mcdonough, P., & Morrissey, P. (2006). Logotherapy as an Adjunctive Treatment for Chronic Combat-related PTSD: A Meaning-based Intervention. American Journal of Psychotherapy, 60(2), 161-174.

Still, A. (2006). Rationality and REBT. *Journal of Cognitive & Behavioral Psychotherapies*, 6(1), 5-10.

Weinrach, S. G., Ellis, A., MacLaren, C., DiGiuseppe, R., Vernon, A., Wolfe, J., & ... Backx, W. (2001). Rational Emotive Behavior Therapy Successes and Failures: Eight Personal Perspectives. *Journal of Counseling & Development*, 79(3), 259.

Weinrach, S. G. (1995). Rational Emotive Behavior Therapy: A Tough-Minded Therapy for a Tender-Minded Profession. *Journal Of Counseling & Development*, 73(3), 296-300.